Fashion Drawing

SECOND EDITION

Patrick John Ireland

Cambridge University Press

CAMBRIDGE
LONDON   NEW YORK   NEW ROCHELLE
MELBOURNE   SYDNEY

About the author
Patrick John Ireland MSIAD is a fashion designer and illustrator. He lectures at the London College of Fashion and is a visiting lecturer to many places in Britain and abroad.

A note on the drawings in this book
Some fashion designs date very swiftly. The drawings in this book have been produced over a period of two years and while some designs are classic and therefore dateless, some reflect the changing mood and style of fashion between 1982 and 1984. Some drawings also reflect the influence of a fashion image from a previous decade which has become prevalent in today's designs.

All drawings by Patrick John Ireland.

The author would like to thank Miss Patricia Wedderburn for her advice on aspects of the fashion industry.

Cover illustrations
The front cover shows three fashion drawings produced with fibre tipped pens of different thicknesses. The three fashion images are shown on page 25 where presentation techniques suitable for competitions, displays and examination assessments are illustrated.

The back cover is a presentation drawing of two evening outfits, drawn with a Rotring pen.

Title page
The fashion sketch shown in two stages was produced with a fine Pentel fibre tipped pen. The tone and colour effects were done with coloured magic marker pens.

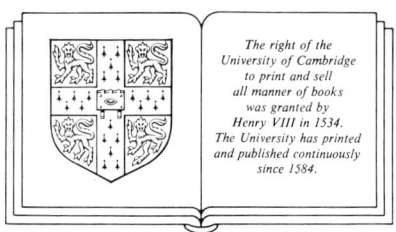

The right of the University of Cambridge to print and sell all manner of books was granted by Henry VIII in 1534. The University has printed and published continuously since 1584.

Published by the Press Syndicate of the University of Cambridge
The Pitt Building, Trumpington Street, Cambridge CB2 1RP
32 East 57th Street, New York, NY 10022, USA
296 Beaconsfield Parade, Middle Park, Melbourne 3206, Australia

© Cambridge University Press 1980, 1984

First published 1980
Reprinted 1982
Second edition 1984

Printed in Great Britain by
David Green Printers Ltd, Kettering

ISBN 0 521 26916 4
(First edition ISBN 0 521 21994 9)

Contents

Introduction *p 3*
Basic figure drawing *p 5*
Creating designs using a figure guide *p 8*
Artists' materials *p 10*
How to draw fabrics *p 12*
The design development sheet *p 16*
Drawing details *p 18*
Production drawing *p 22*
Presentation drawing *p 24*
Heads and hairstyles *p 28*
Drawing accessories *p 30*
Mounting and presenting work *p 31*
The fashion industry *p 31*
Further reading *p 32*

Introduction

In order to develop his ideas, the fashion designer needs a style of drawing that is clear, fluent and adaptable. He also needs to be able to use his fashion sketches to convey his ideas to those responsible for making up his designs into garments to sell.

This book introduces some of the basic principles of fashion drawing. Together with its companion *Fashion Design* it is intended to help students beginning fashion and design courses to develop the skills of creating and communicating design ideas. Many of the sections in this book include drawing and research assignments which will provide the student with the practice he needs in translating ideas into initial sketches and in developing the different styles of drawing required when working as a fashion designer.

The process of fashion design

The fashion designer can either work freelance, designing and producing his own garments and selling them directly to shops, or he can work for clothes manufacturers freelance, or he can be employed full time by a particular clothes manufacturer. In the last case he will work in a design studio with a team of designers and machinists (whose job it is to make up sample garments). The number of staff employed and the stages of the design process vary according to the size and organisation of the company. The following outline is one example of how a design could evolve from the initial design brief to the completed mass-produced garment in the factory.

1. The design brief
Designers usually work from a written brief which specifies
(*a*) the type of garment, or collection of garments required (e.g. summer or winter wear, sportswear or evening wear, coordinated separates etc.);
(*b*) the retail outlet and price range. The proposed price of a garment and where it is to be sold will dictate the designer's ideas about the quality and amount of fabric and trimmings he uses. He must also consider the time and skill which will be involved in making up the garment.

Before a design team begins work on a new season's collection, members will meet to discuss the styles, fabrics and colours in vogue for the coming season.

2. Selection of fabrics
These may be supplied by the manufacturer with the design brief, or the designer may select them himself from a textile manufacturer's range. The choice has to be made early in the design process so that the fabric is delivered in good time.

Sample lengths of the chosen fabrics are ordered to make up sample garments. If the suggested fabrics are very expensive, then a toile (a design made up in a cheap cotton) will be produced instead.

3. Design development
Having selected the fabrics and decided on the colours, patterns and textures for his collection, the designer usually starts to produce sheets of sketches. The sketches are produced very rapidly, experimenting with ideas on a particular theme, adapting the designs and working out the details and colour combinations. Occasionally, the designer may produce some rough design ideas before he chooses the fabrics.

4. Selection of designs for sample garments
In collaboration with his colleagues the designer chooses the most successful designs from his sketches. Patterns are then cut for making sample garments in the chosen fabrics.

5. Selection of trimmings
At this stage the designer must consider the co-ordination of his fabrics with any trimmings such as quilting, embroidery, appliqué, etc. which may be produced by an outside firm. The designer takes great care in his selection of buttons, clasps, buckles and other fastenings and trimmings because they must be an integral part of his overall design.

6. Viewing the sample garments
When the machinists have made the sample garments the designers, manufacturing team and sales staff meet to consider the success and viability of the designs. Sample-machinists are trained to report on any parts of a garment which have proved difficult to assemble. Adjustments are often made at this stage to the fitting and trimmings. The team then decides which designs to manufacture.

7. Costing
A costing is usually done in the design department, based on an estimate of how much time each operation in the making of the garment will take and the costs of the fabrics and trimmings. Any economies which are needed to maintain the proposed price are made at this stage.

8. Production sample
Once the final design is decided, a production sample is made at the factory. Here, the most economical sequence of production is considered and again the garment may have to be modified if the production cost works out to be too high.

The manufacturer's design and production teams approve the completed production sample and the final quantity for production, and the range of colours and sizes is then fixed.

9. Hard pattern
A production pattern is made from a thick card and graded into the different sizes. Before bulk cutting begins it is usually necessary to experiment with the pattern layout to find the most economical way of cutting the pattern pieces from the material.

10. Marketing
A sales conference takes place to discuss sales outlets and advertising. A sample garment of each design in a collection is made up and shown to buyers at fashion shows a few months before the selling season begins.

11. Quality control
Garments are inspected before they leave the factory to ensure the manufacture is up to the required standard.

The uses of fashion drawing

There are three stages in the process outlined above at which a fashion designer needs to be able to execute different styles of drawing. As a student it is important to develop your skills in all three types of drawing.

Design development
At the earliest stage of developing a design, the designer's sketches will be fairly rough, exploring and experimenting with the many possibilities from one central idea or theme. The sheets of sketches produced at this stage are known as design development sheets.

For design sketching the beginner requires practice in drawing figures, fashion garments and design details. Design development sheets are often very helpful to teachers and examiners as they give a clear insight into the way a student has developed his ideas and his method of working.

Design development sheet for casual sportswear. A designer would continue to work on this theme making several sheets of drawings before selecting designs to take to the next stage. Look how this designer has drawn details such as pockets and waist fastenings separately, in order to think through his ideas. (A 1979–80 fashion image.)

Production drawing
When the design for a garment has been approved by the design and marketing departments and a sample is requested, the production team will need a specification sheet and a production drawing of the design.

This drawing has to be clear and diagrammatic in order to show details of the cut, seam and dart placement and proposed style features. Detailed production drawings are also needed for the final design specification which goes to the factory where the garments are to be made.

As a student you will need to spend time studying how garments are put together so that you can represent the structure of garments in your production drawings clearly and accurately.

Presentation drawing
Presentation drawings are used to present a collection of design ideas to buyers. They should be finished drawings which project the intended fashion image of the collection. This means that you must give careful thought not only to drawing the garments themselves, but also to the pose of

the figures, the hairstyles and accessories, in order to achieve an attractive and eye-catching overall effect. You will also need to practise using colour in your drawing; presentation drawings should represent accurately the colours of the fabrics you have chosen for your designs.

This presentation drawing was produced on smooth white card with a fine lead HB Pentel propelling pencil. The halftone wash was added with a grey watercolour. Note the pose of the two figures and the way they have been arranged to achieve a pleasing composition, while giving the full effect and detail of the garments' design.

The fashion illustrator

The fashion illustrator is trained as a graphic designer. His job is to illustrate and promote the work of the fashion designer by producing fashion sketches for newspapers, magazines, catalogues, exhibitions and window displays. He usually develops his own distinctive style of drawing by which he is known.

Some fashion designers do also work as fashion illustrators. However, as fashion illustration is usually taught as a separate subject in colleges, this book is not intended to cover this particular aspect of fashion drawing.

Basic figure drawing

In order to have scope to express your design ideas precisely and to present them attractively, you need first of all to develop skill in figure drawing. You should be able to sketch the figure from memory in a number of different poses.

At first you will need to work hard at figure drawing so that you can memorise the normal proportions of the figure and draw freehand figures with confidence. It is a good idea to attend life drawing and costume life classes to practise. However, as this is not always possible, the methods illustrated in this book will help you develop your technique.

The height of the average figure varies between 7½ and 8 times the length of the head. It is advisable to keep to these normal figure proportions when designing. The more exaggerated poses and figure proportions like some of those shown on the inside covers are usually only used in presentation drawings and fashion advertising to promote a particular fashion image.

Start by drawing the figure following the three stages illustrated. First draw a grid which gives the overall figure length divided into seven and a half head lengths. Then draw vertical construction lines from the second line to the bottom line and horizontal construction lines (to show where the shoulders and hips will come) between the second and third, and fourth and fifth lines. Then sketch in the figures around these construction lines. Do not make the construction or grid lines too heavy; they are only meant to serve as a guide while drawing the figure. Check the position of the chin, bust and waist and the overall proportions of your drawing against the drawing in the book.

You should keep your figure simple to start with — only suggest the hair, face, hands and feet until you have had time to practise and gain more confidence. Even this simple pose of a front and back view will enable you to develop your own design ideas for garments and to present them clearly. Later, as you become more experienced at figure drawing, you can develop numerous different figure poses from this method.

It is also important to practise sketching the figure freehand as well as around a grid. You can improve at this by sketching from a model.

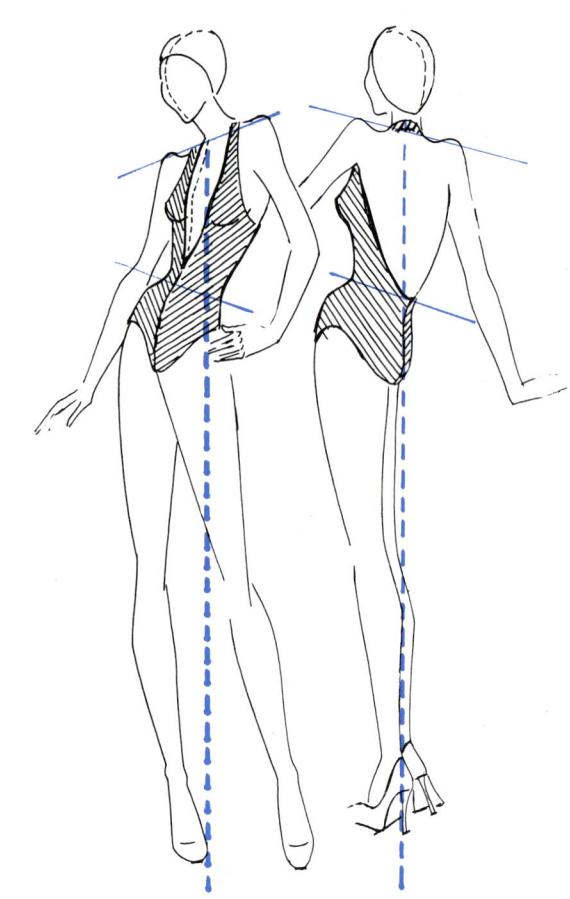

Develop the pose by changing the angle of the hips and shoulders.

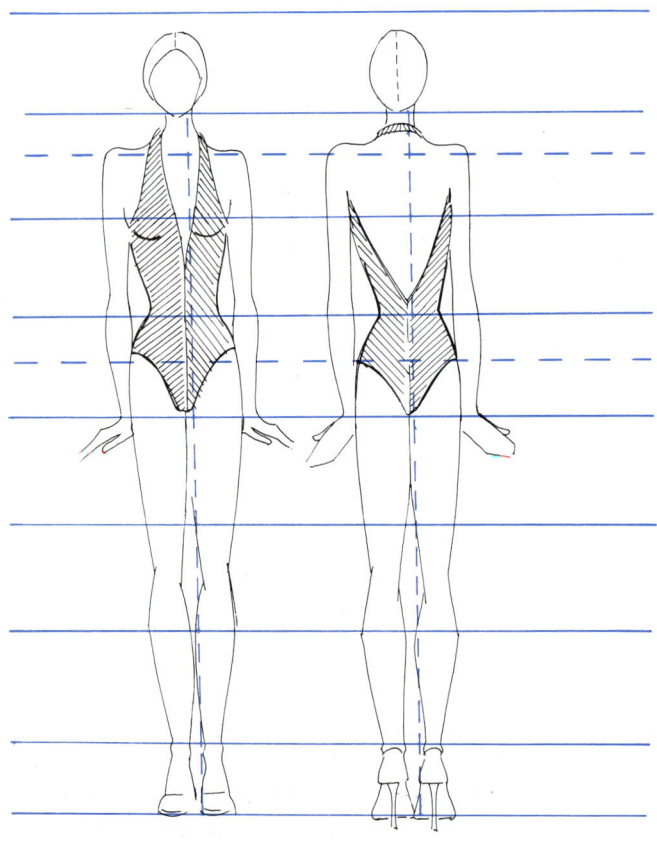

Basic figure guide.

Note the balance line falling from the pit of the neck to the foot which takes the weight of the body.

6

Look at the angle of the hips and shoulders when the figure is standing with the weight on one leg and the effect this has on the angle of the hemline and the position of the centre front and back lines of the skirt.

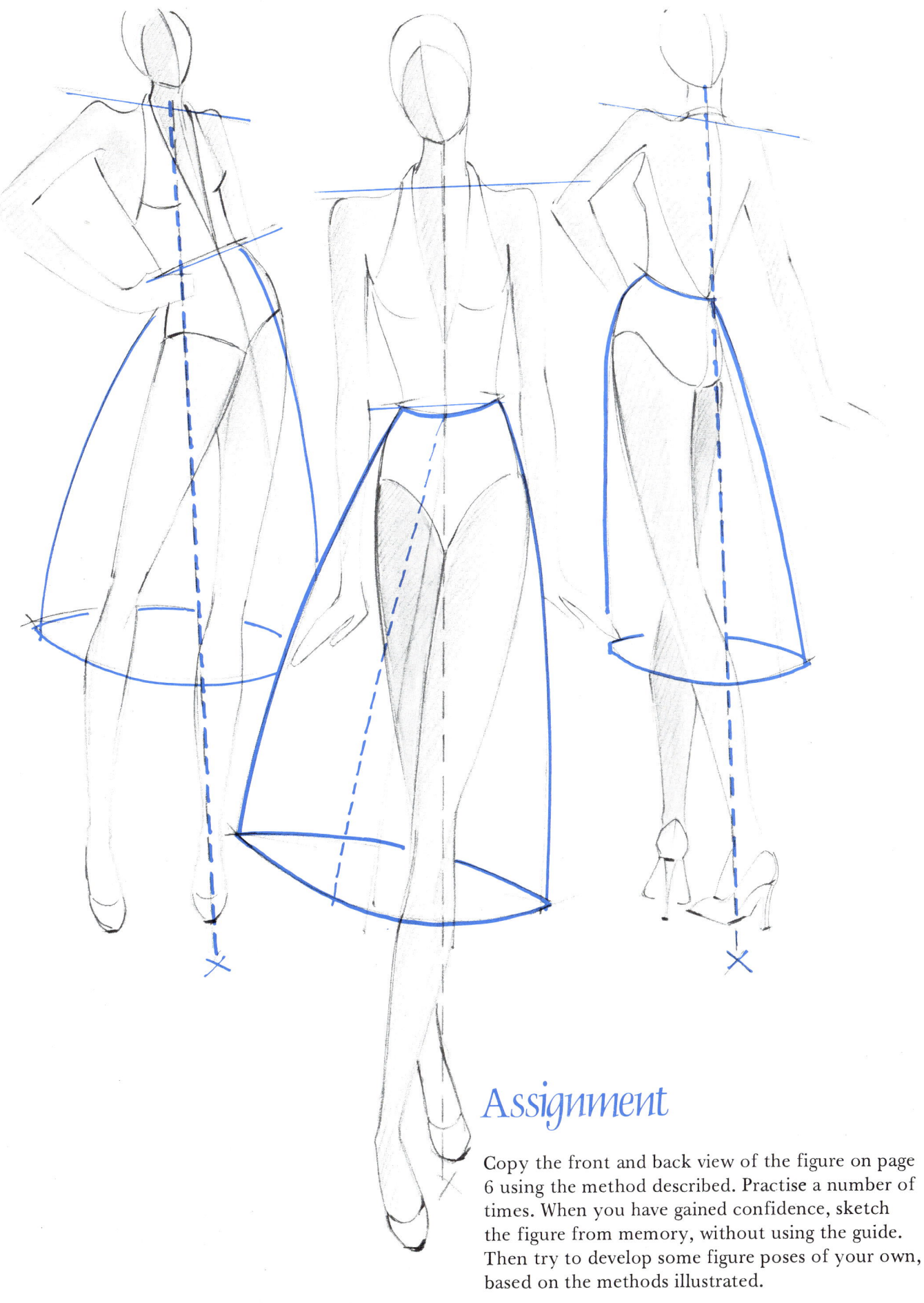

Assignment

Copy the front and back view of the figure on page 6 using the method described. Practise a number of times. When you have gained confidence, sketch the figure from memory, without using the guide. Then try to develop some figure poses of your own, based on the methods illustrated.

Creating designs using a figure guide

If you continue to find drawing the figure difficult when designing it is useful to follow the three stages illustrated here. You can either trace the figure poses from this page or from inside the front or back covers of this book or, preferably, construct your own figures from these illustrations. Then follow the stages shown to draw the garments over the figure guides. The coloured lines will help you to see how this has been done.

You can use this technique of drawing garments over a figure guide to develop your own design ideas. If you draw a series of simple figures in front and back view, as shown on page 9, you can create a variety of designs for a garment and so make a very simple design development sheet.

Assignment

Design three simple summer dresses, using a thin semi-transparent paper placed over the figure guides which you drew in your previous assignment (page 7).

Remember to design around the outline of the figure and to take account of the fabric you have selected. Think about the way the material would gather and fall.

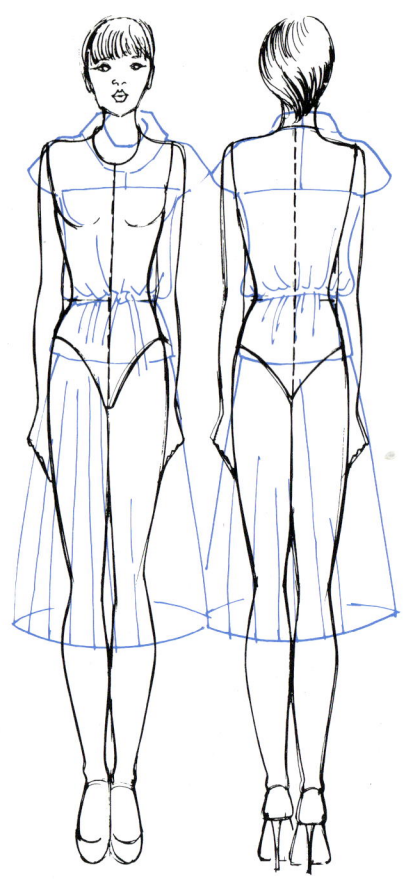

Stage two: place layout paper over the figure guide and sketch your design for the garment.

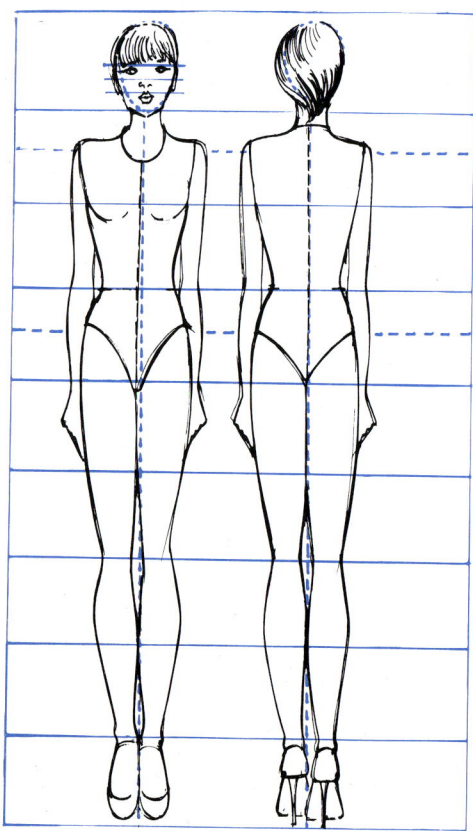

Stage one: sketch the figure guide.

Stage three: complete the details of the sketch, remembering to relate them to the proportions of the figure.

A design development sheet which uses a simple method to convey several design ideas around one theme. The designs were produced on semi-transparent layout paper placed over the figure guides.

Note the variations of the initial idea achieved by changing the sleeve and waist shape. The sketches were drawn with a black Pentel pen and the colour applied with a felt pen.

Designers often attach sample fabrics to their design sketches when they are showing them to colleagues or potential clients.

Artists' materials

As a student you will need to experiment with different drawing materials. A large selection of papers, paints, pastels and pens can be bought in any good art shop. You should work with new materials whenever possible and experiment with new techniques. It is not always necessary to spend a lot of money to achieve the best results.

Listed below are some of the basic materials you will need and some of the more sophisticated ones you may like to try out when you become more experienced.

Types of paper

Cartridge paper is white and has a finely grained surface suitable for pencil, paint, crayon and charcoal. It is made in several different thicknesses and qualities.

Coloured cartridge paper has a slightly textured surface and is suitable for watercolour, pastels, and coloured pencils.

Cartridge drawing pads with stiff cardboard backs are obtainable in a range of sizes.

Cartridge sketch pads have stiff cardboard backs and throw over covers.

Layout pads contain white semi-transparent detail paper with a surface ideal for pencil, ink or crayon.

Watercolour paper is especially made for watercolour painting and can have either a smooth or a rough surface. Many different qualities are available in pad or book form.

Ingres paper is ideal for pastel and tempera work. You can buy a large selection of colours in sheets or as a pad.

Bound sketch books are made in different sizes and qualities of paper.

Illustration board is available in different sizes and thicknesses with a variety of surfaces which will take ink, gouache, watercolour, charcoal and crayon.

Coloured mounting board is a smooth dull-surfaced board suitable for mounting work. A large selection of colours is available in different sizes and thicknesses.

Bristol board has a smooth white surface suitable for pen and ink work.

Drawing pens

Many different drawing pens are available. Listed below are a few of them, selected for their different effects.

Rotring technical pens have a drawing point which may be replaced with different sizes. They are designed for easy refilling.

The Pelikan Technos drawing pen is a cartridge filled drawing pen with points designed for different types of art work e.g. stencilling, ruling and free-hand work.

Osmiroid Sketch fountain pens are less expensive pens which provide a variety of line values from bold to fine. The pens are fitted with reservoirs to maintain constant ink flow.

Pen holders and nibs. A selection of plastic or wood pen holders and different sized nibs are made for use with coloured or black indian ink and are cheaper than the other pens listed.

Pencils

Drawing pencils. A pencil's degree of hardness is printed on it in a standard code: 6B is very soft; 9H is very hard; F and HB are medium; EX is extremely soft.

Charcoal pencils will give the same effect as pure charcoal sticks. They are non-scratch and non-glossy and are available in hard, medium and soft.

Coloured pencils can be bought in boxes or separately in a wide range of colours. Some makes are water soluble which enables you to wash over the pencil stroke with a paint brush giving the effect of painting.

Crayons

Wax crayons can be most effective in fashion sketches. There is a good selection of colours and thicknesses.

Erasers

Kneaded erasers are soft putty rubbers that can be moulded to a point, and used for pastel, charcoal and pencil.

Soft erasers are used for pencil lead or surface cleaning.

Paper cleaner or gum eraser is a pliable soft eraser gum which wears away during use but does not damage the paper surface.

Marker pens

There are two basic types: spirit and water. The line thicknesses can vary from very fine to broad. The tips are either nylon, fibre or felt.

Magic markers are made in many colours and are quick drying. The ink flows smoothly through a wedge-shaped felt nib. Colours can be mixed by superimposition. Fine-line markers are also available in corresponding colours.

Stabilo fibre tips come in a good range of colours with a shaped tip to give you a fine line used upright and a broad side for filling in large areas. Available in sets or individually.

Design drawings using different techniques: from left to right the materials used are Rotring pen; fibre tipped pen and grey magic marker; and Pentel pencil with a fine lead.

Colour

Pastels are obtainable in a large range of colours and different qualities. The prices vary with the quality.

Designers gouache colours, sold in tubes, are excellent for their outstanding brilliance and exceptionally smooth flow. They will produce combinations of transparency and opacity.

Drawing inks. All inks can be used equally well with brush or pen and may be diluted with distilled water. Because they contain shellac a second coat may be superimposed without disturbing the first.

Watercolours. Boxes of students' or artists' watercolours are sold in a range of sizes, and are also sold in tubes.

Adhesives

Cow Gum is a transparent rubber solution sold in tubes or tins for mounting photographs and pasting up work.

Pritt is a non-greasy adhesive, suitable for sticking fabric.

Copydex, an extra strong latex adhesive, is suitable for paper and fabric.

Spray Mount is sold in aerosol cans for mounting work. It gives an instant all over tack and wrinkle-free bond even on the thinnest paper. Mounted work can be unstuck.

Photo Mount is a permanent adhesive for mounting photographs which is colourless, quick to apply and easy to control.

Protective sprays

It is often a good idea to protect your work against accidental damage with a protective spray. The spray effects are either matt or glossy.

Brushes

The best quality brushes are still made by hand which means they are very expensive. Many sizes and qualities are available from sable hair and ox hair, to squirrel which is cheaper. Hog hair is used to make brushes for oil painting because of its strength and ability to hold oil paint. More recently cheaper synthetic hair brushes have become available. Always clean your brushes immediately after use. Shape up the hairs after cleaning and never leave brushes resting on their bristles.

Portfolios

Stiff durable portfolios are made from resistant simulated fabric. The corners, gusset and the hinged flaps are reinforced with strong cloth.

Black leathercloth portfolios, with zip closing are used by professional designers — the work is displayed in transparent pockets which are held in a ring binder.

Presentation books have hard plastic covers and contain clear acetate pockets. They are used for protecting and displaying work.

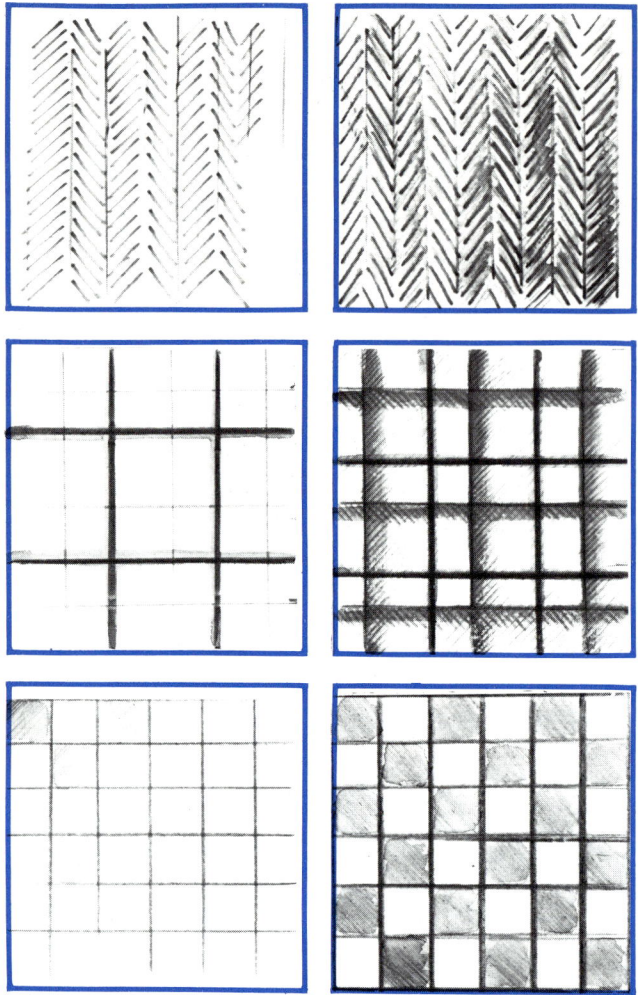

A variety of media used to achieve the effects of different fabric textures — top: herringbone tweed; centre: tartan; bottom: check.

How to draw fabrics

Study the behaviour of different fabrics. Look at the way in which they drape, gather, pleat and fall into folds. When you have the opportunity to handle lengths of fabric, drape them on a dressmaker's model using pins. Try to create several different effects. Make sketches of the folds and drapes. Observe the different qualities of lengths of chiffon, velvet or tweed, for example. Keep your sketches; they can be useful for reference when you are drawing a particular fabric.

Collect samples of fabrics that appeal to you. These can be used later when developing design sheets.

Pencil fashion sketch of garments in soft materials, incorporating folds and gathers as a feature of the design.

Assignments

1. Keep a collection of pens, pencils, crayons etc. for experimenting with. Practise achieving the effects of different fabrics, suggesting colour and pattern, texture and weave by mixing your media.

Take sheets of different papers of various weight, texture and colour. Draw a number of boxes as illustrated and try to create different patterns, textures and colourwash effects in each box.

Collect sample pieces of fabric of different textures and patterns to copy from. Keep the results for future reference when designing.
2. Sketch a number of figures in a selection of garments, e.g. dresses, coats, suits, furs. Practise applying to the drawings the different effects of texture and patterns learnt in Assignment 1.

Three stages of producing a design sketch, showing how to draw folds and gathers. Note the use of construction lines and the balance of the hem lines. (A classic fashion 1983.)

Assignments

1. Design three dresses in soft, plain materials. Use gathers, drapes and folds as features of the design. Consider carefully the quality of the fabrics you have chosen and the way in which the material behaves when draped and gathered.
2. Design three evening dresses in fabric selected for its drape and pattern. Study carefully the way in which the fabric falls into folds and the effect this has on the pattern.

Practise suggesting the patterns first, then add them to your designs. Remember to keep the pattern in scale with the figure. When applying a pattern or texture to a garment you have drawn decide on which side you want to indicate the light falling and work the pattern or shading on the other side of the figure.

Patterns and textures

When drawing the textures and patterns of different fabrics it is important to study the fabrics themselves in order to decide how best to represent them in your design drawing. It is a good idea to experiment with different media before finally choosing the drawing technique and materials you are going to use.

When you want to represent more than one fabric within a design drawing you will probably need to use several different drawing techniques and materials to achieve the contrast of texture between the different fabrics. Remember to relate the pattern and representation of texture to the scale of the drawing.

When drawing figures in movement note how the fabric falls and the behaviour of the folds and gathers. These sketches were drawn with a Royal Sovereign Black Prince pencil.

right: Fashion sketch illustrating a selection of different surface effects and textures incorporated in one design. The blouse was drawn with a fine pointed HB pencil with a grey watercolour wash added. The effect of fur for the waistcoat was achieved with paint applied with a dry brush. The tweed skirt was drawn in black wax crayon applied with varying pressure.

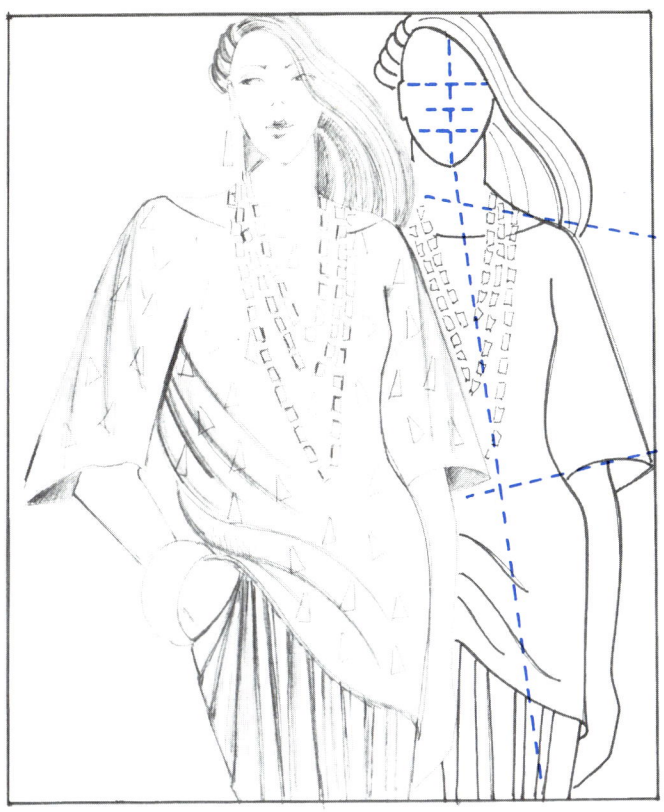

These fashion sketches were drawn in two stages. Look at the way in which the patterns have been suggested. A fine lead Pentel pencil was used in the drawing of the outfit above to suggest the softness of the fabric.

The dress was drawn with a very fine pen (Rotring pen) to suggest a very flimsy material.

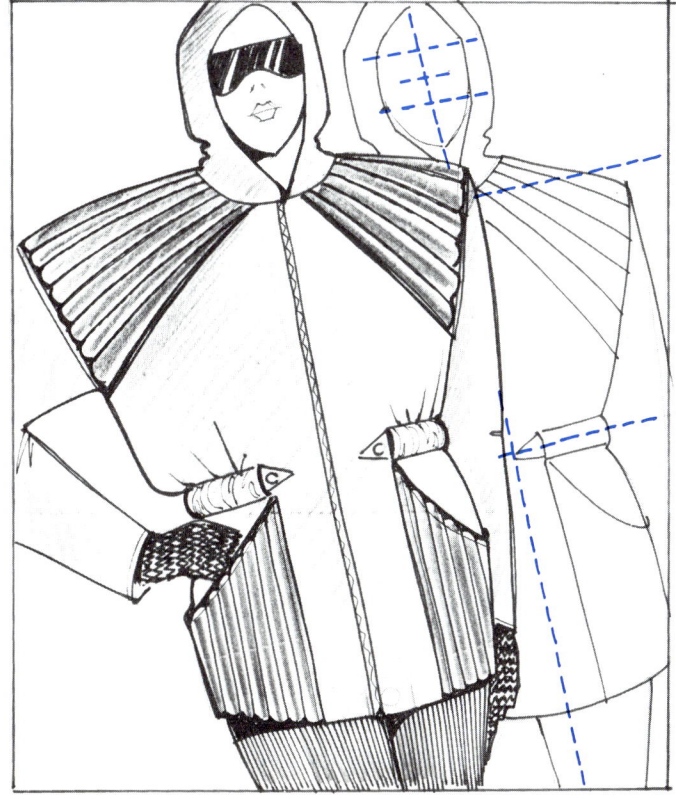

The ski jacket was drawn with a black fibre tipped pen and black pencil was used for the shading to suggest quilting.

Assignment

Keep a collection of interesting patterned fabrics for reference. Practise drawing and painting them using different media, combining the effects of coloured pencils, paints, inks, felt pens etc. Indicate the balance of colour and tones of the pattern and remember to draw it to scale. Before you begin it is helpful to look at the fabric with half-closed eyes. This gives the overall impression of the pattern which is the effect you will need for your fashion sketch.

The design development sheet

The design development sheet is a designer's starting point when designing a garment or a collection of garments. The designer begins work by producing a series of sketches, developing one particular idea in a number of different ways. He will then use the most successful design development sheets to present his design ideas to colleagues or clients.

The style of drawing you use for design development needs to be free enough to experiment swiftly and confidently with a variety of alternative design features for the garment you are working on but clear enough to communicate your ideas convincingly to colleagues or clients.

Start by producing a series of sketches working on a particular theme suggested by the design brief you have been given. Experiment with all the possibilities of the idea, including small sketches of design details on the sheet as well as alternative designs for the whole garment. Do not forget to think about the design for the back of the garment as well as the front.

It is often helpful to have chosen the fabric for which you are designing before you start sketching out your ideas. A length of fabric draped, with the aid of a few pins, on a dress stand is often an excellent source of inspiration. Also, you can look at the way the fabric behaves when gathered, pleated or folded and take this into consideration when designing.

Sometimes it is useful to make up a fabric board of the colours, textures and patterns you have selected. Pin all the fabrics you have chosen for a collection of garments or an outfit, together with any trimmings and rough sketches, on a board on the studio wall. This will help you to see how the fabrics look together.

You can also use small samples of the materials you have chosen to experiment with different surface effects, such as smocking, shirring and quilting.

Developing your own designs around a given design brief will involve rejecting some ideas and experimenting further with others. Always keep working on one idea until you have completely exhausted all its possibilities. You will soon develop your own individual style and technique for expressing ideas on paper.

Should you have difficulty with figure drawing to begin with, use the guides on the inside front and back covers and on p. 6 of this book. Try out some of the alternative drawing materials and techniques suggested on pp. 10 and 11. Add colour to your design sketches and try to indicate in your drawing the textures and patterns of the fabrics you have chosen. Experiment with colour schemes on a separate sheet before you add colour to the design sheet.

If your work is going to be assessed by a teacher or examiner it is better to produce your series of sketches on separate sheets of paper rather than in a sketch book. This makes the work easy to handle and display.

Assignment

Produce a design development sheet of ideas for a collection of casual summer holiday clothes. Develop the ideas working on a theme. Attach suitable fabrics to the sheet and any notes on the design you think necessary.

A selection of skirts and tops. Note the way in which the striped fabric has been used to introduce a contrast in the design. The drawings were done with an HB Pentel pencil and a coloured felt pen.

Variations of a design for a coat introducing different pockets, collars and sleeves. The design sheet illustrates the complete fashion image (right) combined with line drawings adapting the design. Note also the back views, fabric samples and descriptive notes. The drawings were produced with a thick black pencil combined with a fine Artline 200 pen. (A 1983–4 fashion image.)

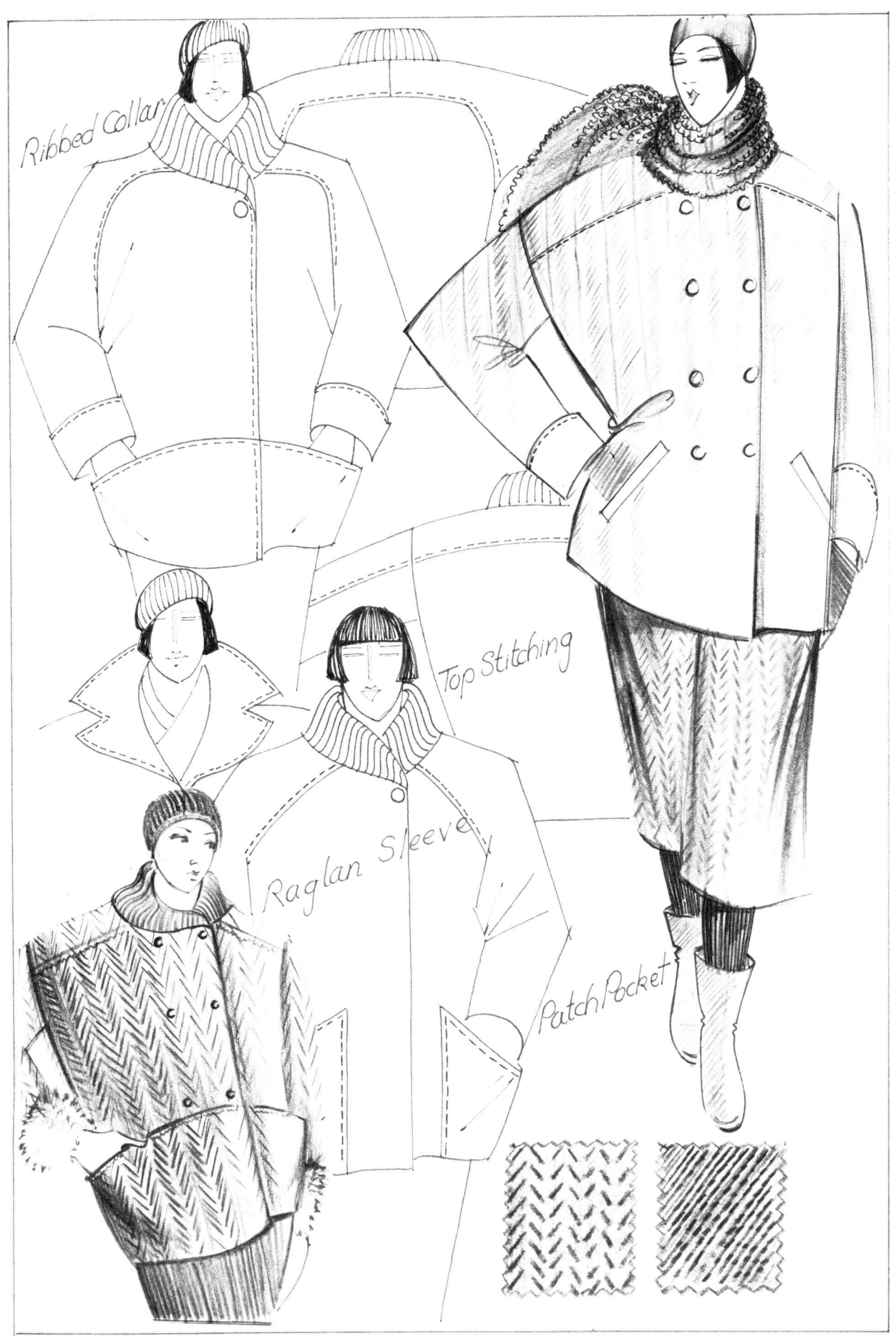

Drawing details

When developing designs, it is important that you understand how the garment you are drawing would be constructed in order to draw it accurately. As you learn more about the cut and make up of garments your technique of sketching sleeves, collars, pleats and other complicated design features will improve. Sketching the shape of a sleeve, the cut of a bodice or a collar, for instance, requires careful observation and practice. You should try to show these details clearly in your sketches.

Assignment

Choose a design feature such as a sleeve, collar or waistband and develop a variety of design possibilities for that feature in your sketch book. Keep the sketches for future reference.

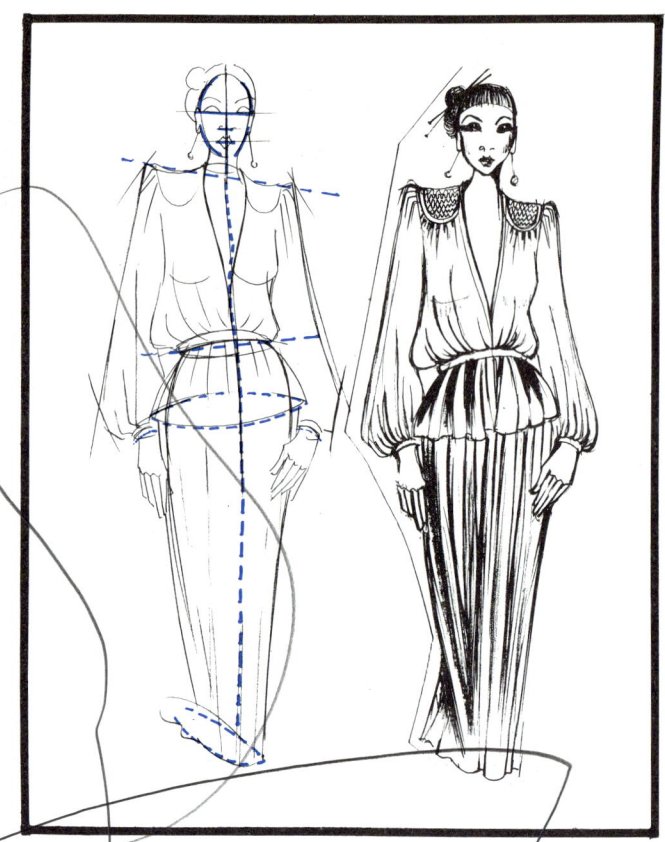

The design details of this evening dress — the shirring within the yoke panels on the shoulders, the peplum at the waist and the soft folds and gathers — are clearly shown in this sketch.

Two stages of producing a fashion sketch. Notice how the collar is placed round the neck and how the details of the blouson jacket — the extended shoulders, the band at the hem — and the blouse have been drawn.

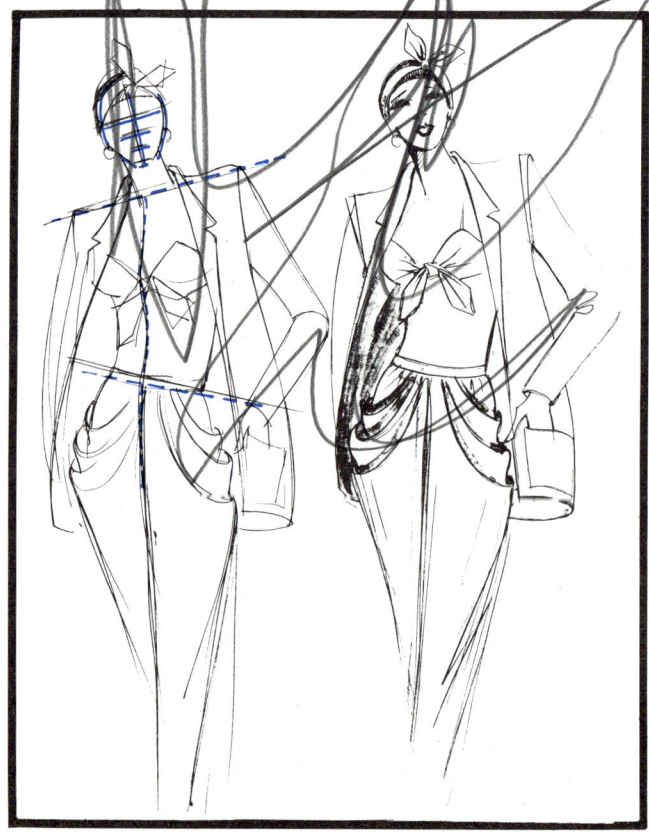

In this outfit notice how the proportions of the narrow jacket collar, the extended shoulders, and the drape of the trousers are suggested.

A selection of sleeves illustrating the construction of the drawing in two stages. Note the fine lines used to sketch the arm, and how the sleeve is sketched round the arm.

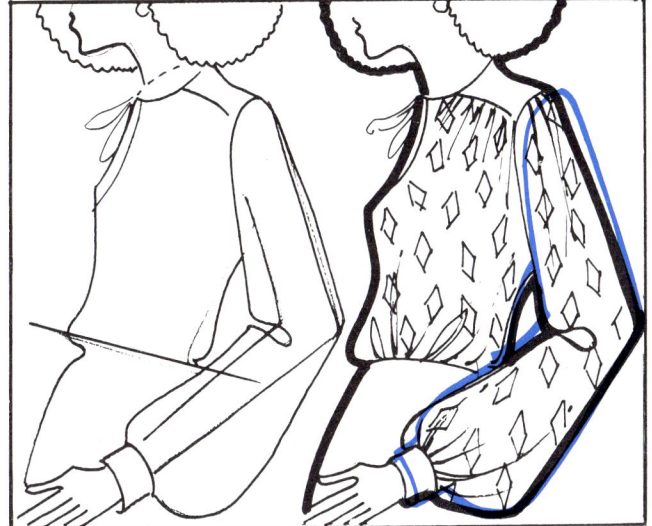

Bishop sleeve

Raglan sleeve

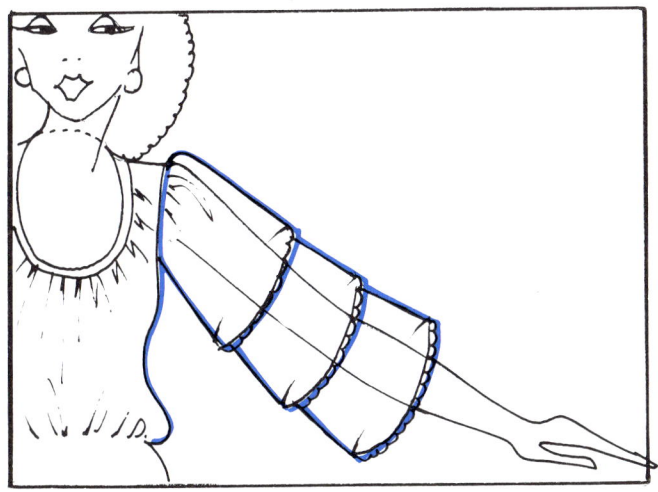

Full layered sleeve

Kimono sleeve

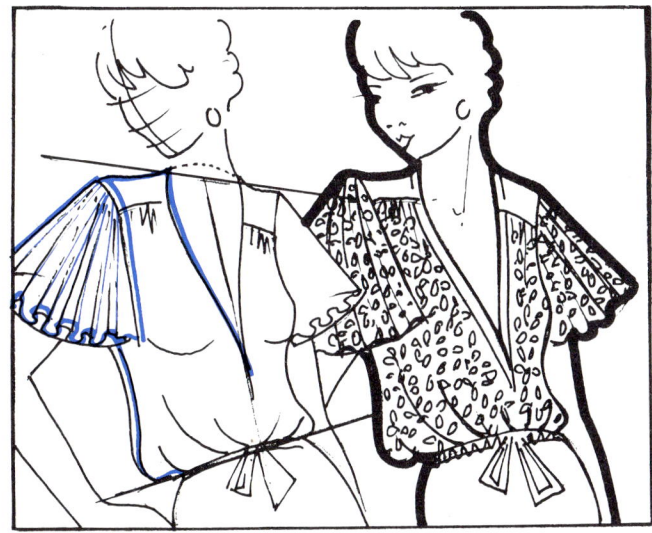

Full circular set-in sleeve

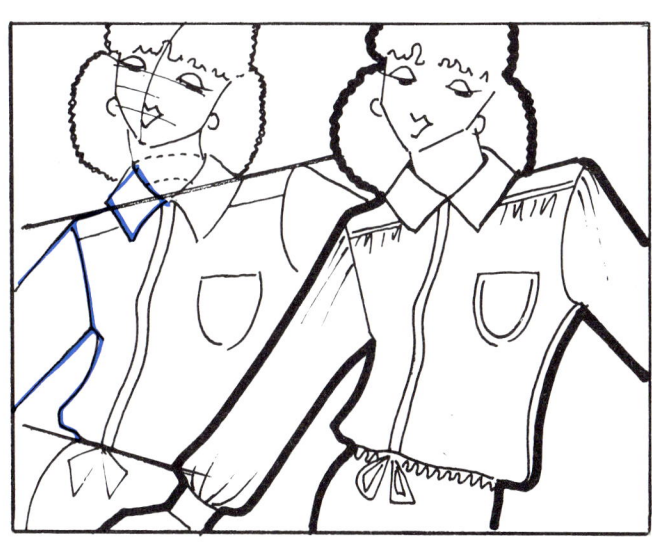

Shirt sleeve with cuff and button fastening

Collars

Collars can often be difficult to draw accurately. Try to make sure that the two sides of the collar and the lapels balance each other and that the collar looks as though it fits round the neck. Many collar designs can be created from the three basic styles: the stand, the roll and the flat collar. As well as being a decorative design feature, the collar often serves the practical purpose of protecting the wearer from the elements.

A selection of collars: the coloured line in the first sketch of each pair helps to indicate how the collar is made.

Assignment

Keep a sketch book of detail drawings for reference. Make sketches of any interesting details which you think add impact to the overall effect of a design. Study magazines, looking closely at the fashion details on a variety of garments and develop some ideas of your own.

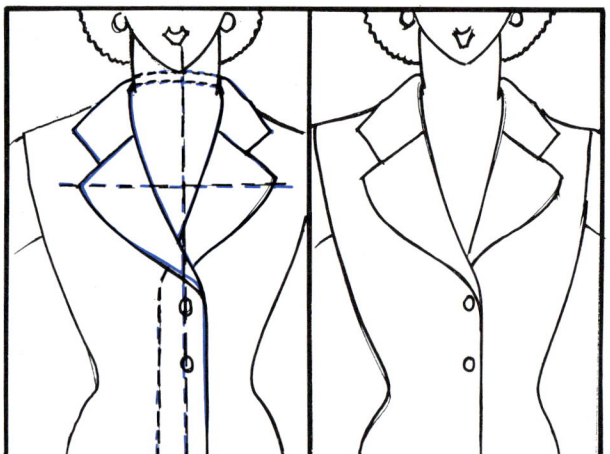
Tailored collar

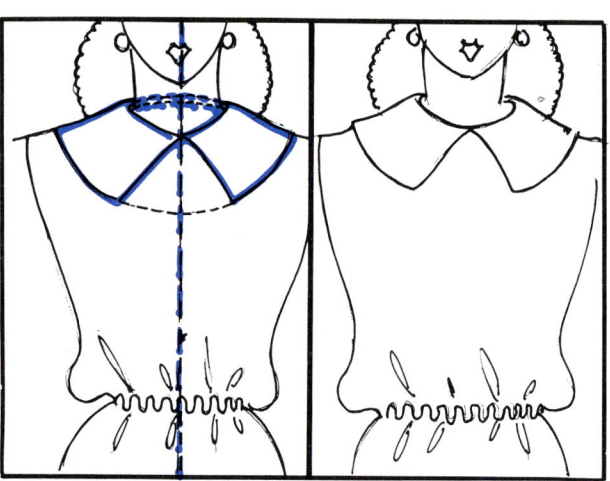
Large flat collar

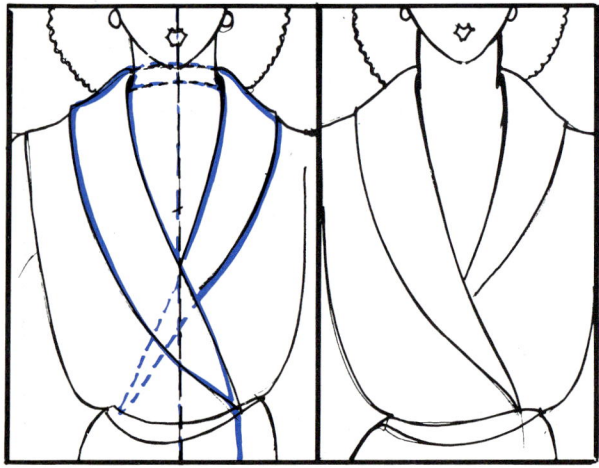
Shawl

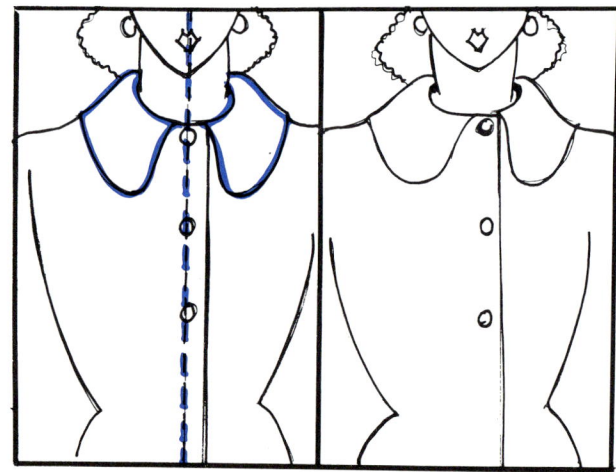
Shaped collar with a roll

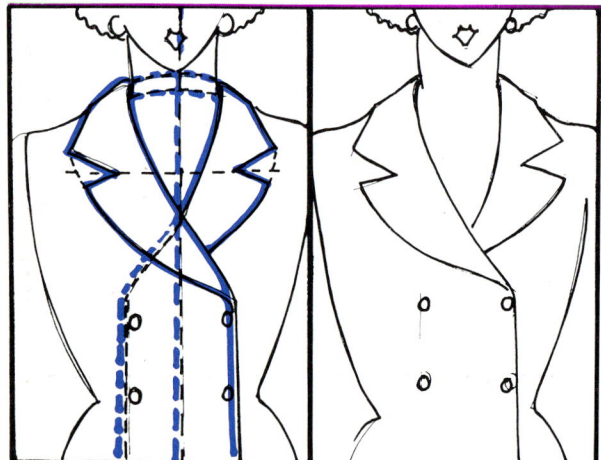
Double-breasted tailored collar

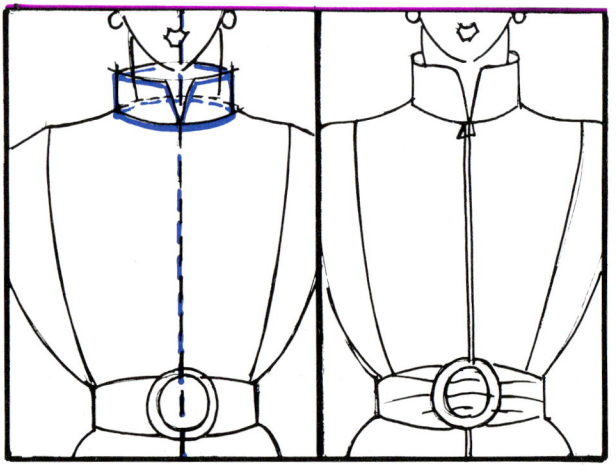
Stand collar

A sample sketch book page showing drawings of different style features and details from a variety of garments.

Production drawing

Once a design for a particular garment has been chosen, a production drawing of the design is needed as a guide for making up the design into a sample garment. If the sample garment is approved and manufacture is to go ahead production drawings are required for the pattern cutter's and machinist's reference.

The style of drawing required for production purposes has to be clear and precise. Drawings should be carefully related to the proportions of the figure, and yokes, pockets, seam-lines and darts must be accurately positioned.

Sheets of information about the cut of the garment and specification for its make up are usually attached to the production drawing. When a garment is going to be mass-produced these sheets are often extremely detailed.

The examples of production drawing illustrated here range from a very simple design to drawings of more complicated and detailed designs.

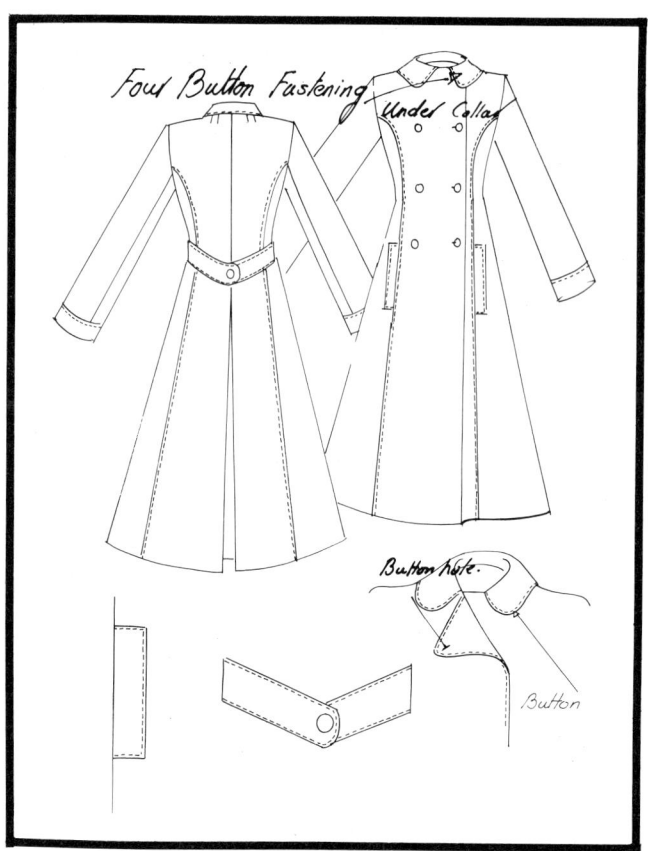

Production drawing for a semi-fitted double-breasted coat with four-button fastening and rounded collar. It has pockets in the side front seams and an unpressed inverted pleat centre back, buttoned half belt, full length sleeves cut on the bias, and decorative topstitching.

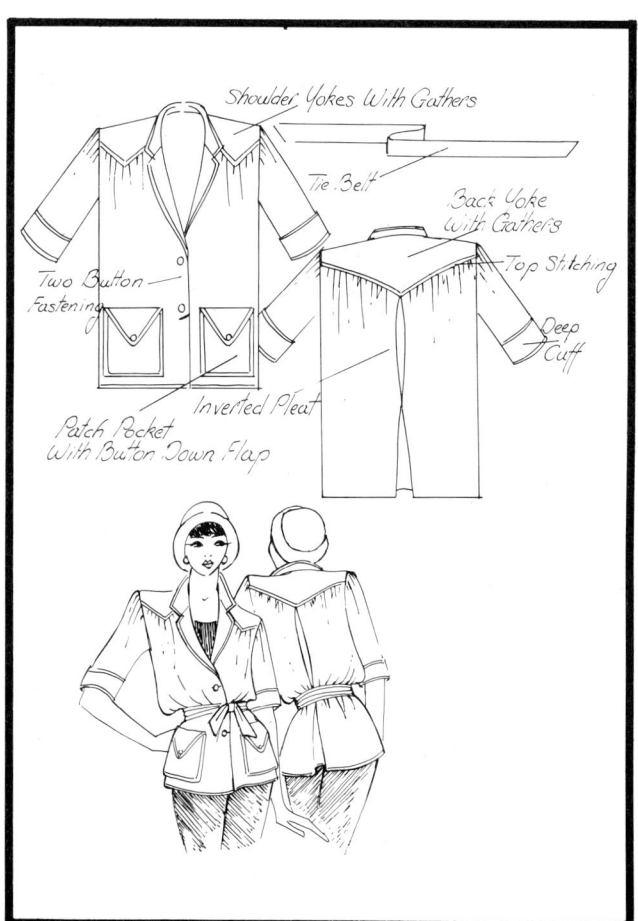

Production drawing for a casual jacket with a gathered yoke front and back, two-button fastening, and inverted pleat centre back. The short sleeves have a loose cuff. Design details include patch pockets with button down flaps, and a belt.

Fitted panel jacket with centre-front four-button fastening, patch pockets, shaped yoke interest and tie belt at waist. Sleeveless fitted blouse with three-button centre-front fastening, shaped collar and lapel worn outside jacket. Trousers cut slightly flared with waist band and button fastening.

Evening dress with coat: the bodice of the dress is gathered from the centre front, centre back and side seams and has narrow shoulder straps. The skirt is full and gathered from the waist. Zip fastener opening at the back of bodice.

The coat is cut very full with gathers from the shoulders. The yokes are decorated with shirring and the sleeves are full, gathered at the wrist with ties.

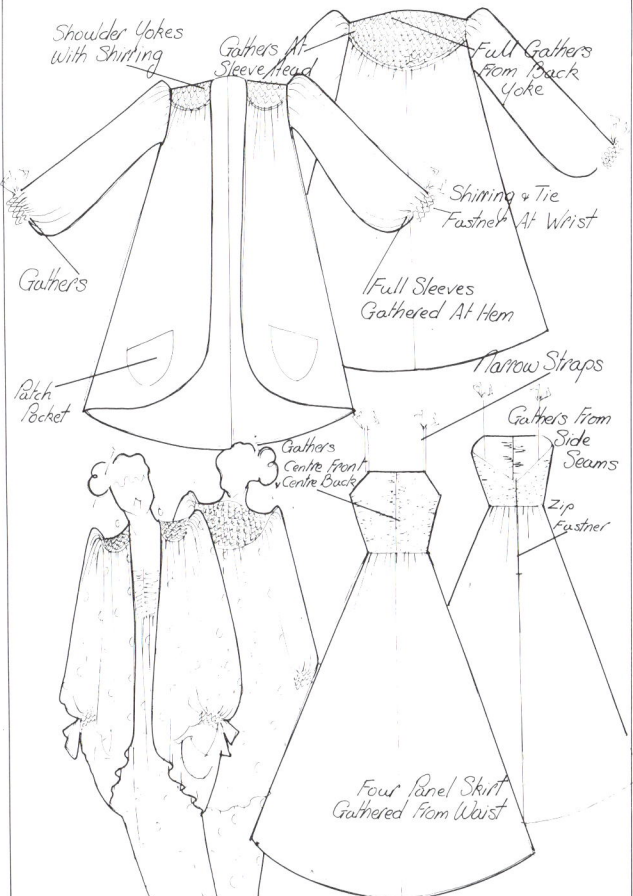

RANGE		STYLE NO.		DESIGN NO.		
CODE	COMPOSITION		WIDTH	YARDAGE	SAMPLE COLOUR	
MAIN MATERIAL						
CONTRAST MATERIAL						
LINING						
INTERLINING						
	DESCRIPTION	SUPPLIER	DESIGN NO.	PRICE	PER YARD	ZIPS	BUTTON HOLES
OUTSIDE PROCESS							
OTHER TRIMMINGS							
	DESCRIPTION	QUANTITY WIDTH	SUPPLIER	DESIGN NO.	LINE BUCKLE	PRICE	
BELT						
BUTTONS						
NOTES						

Specification sheets

Forms called specification or working production sheets are used as guides in the fashion industry when making up garments. The sheet illustrated would give details and prices of the different materials, yardage, trimmings, and lining required. A costing for the garment could be worked out from this sheet.

Another sheet would specify the exact measurements for cutting and making up the garment in different sizes. A production drawing of the garment would be attached to the specification sheet for the pattern cutter's and maker's reference.

Assignments

1. Look carefully at a garment of your choice and make an analytical drawing of it, noting the way in which it has been put together and the placement of darts, seams and fashion features. Draw the details of the collar, pockets and sleeves, clearly and precisely.
2. Take one of your own fashion sketches of a garment and consider the way in which it would be made up. Note the details — the sleeves, collar and openings for example — and the proportions.

After carefully considering the design and construction of the garment make a production drawing of it. Consider how best to arrange the drawing on a sheet of paper.

Presentation drawing

This style of drawing is used when showing a new collection to a client once a sample garment has been made up.

As a student, you will need to do presentation drawings when entering a collection of designs in a competition or when presenting a collection of work for an examination assessment. To produce a presentation drawing successfully, you will need to have gained some experience in drawing and be able to use different media.

The presentation drawing illustrates the front and back views of a garment and in some instances, a side or three-quarter view as well. The back view of the design can be illustrated on a figure or produced in diagrammatic form. Sometimes you may find it helpful to add a few notes about a particular design, to explain hidden or complex features. The fabrics you have chosen for the garments should be attached to the sheet and the colours you use in your drawing should match the sample fabrics as exactly as possible.

The fashion image must be strongly projected through the presentation. The pose of the figure, the accessories and the hairstyle you choose must complement the overall design.

The fabrics must be applied to the sheet with careful consideration of their position in the general layout. In some instances you may want to use a background to add to the impact of your design. However, this should not distract from the garment you are presenting.

Layout of presentation sheets

Before you begin your presentation drawing, make a series of quick sketches (like those shown below) to explore the different ways in which the design could be arranged on the paper.

When deciding on the pose of the figures remember it is important to show the design to its full advantage with the front and back view clearly displayed. It is not always necessary to show the whole of the figure although of course it is when presenting a trouser outfit or a long dress, or skirt.

Decide what size, texture and colour of paper will best suit your purpose. On a separate sheet of the paper you have chosen, experiment with portraying the textures and patterns of the fabric you have chosen for your garments. Also try out colours on this sheet to achieve an exact match with your sample fabrics. For competitions a particular size of drawing is often required, so it is helpful to practise presentation drawing on a variety of sizes of paper.

Think carefully how to balance the display of fabrics and any notes you want to add with the general layout and background. These must not be added as an afterthought.

Three sketches exploring alternative layouts for a presentation sheet. The aim is to project the overall image of the fashion design and to show the back view, fabric samples and descriptive notes.

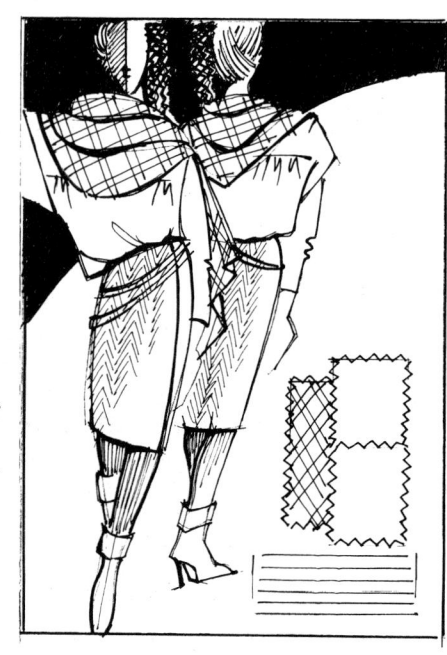

below: The figures are placed together to form a pleasing composition. The background has been filled in with black paint with a band of colour to offset the black and white line drawings. The fabric samples and descriptive notes have been placed where they balance the composition.

right: The figure is shown full length with the back view in line. A section of the sheet has been used to show the fabric samples against a black panel.

below right: Here the figure is placed off centre in colour, and the back view is placed behind as a line drawing. The background has been filled in with black paint. A section has been used in the bottom right corner to display the fabric sample and notes.

A layered look in three jersey fabrics. The top is cut very loose with a drawstring neckline and co-ordinated with a layered skirt of contrasting fabrics, gathered into soft folds.

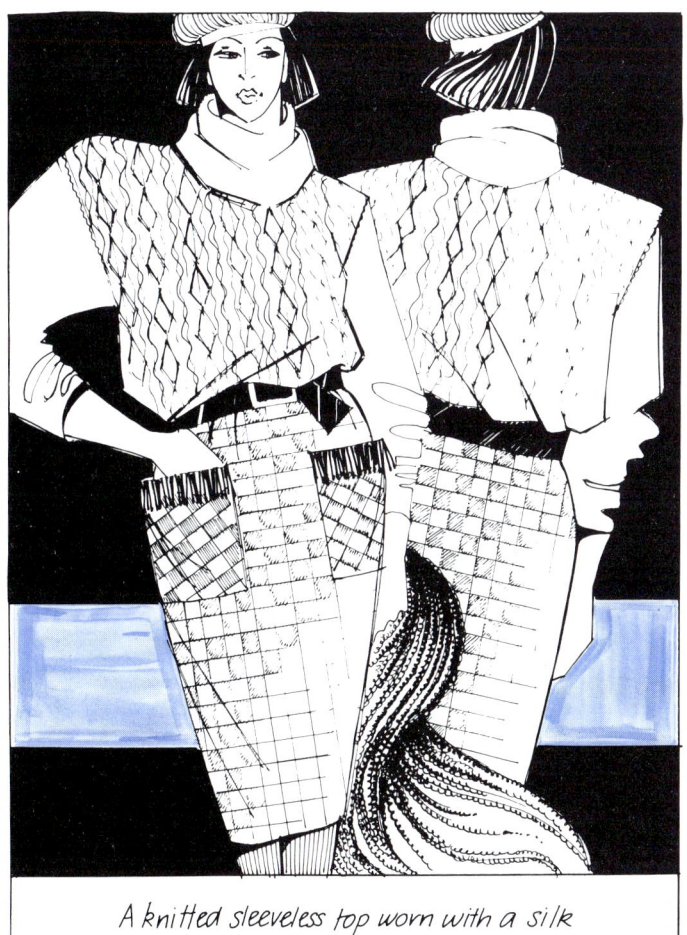

A knitted sleeveless top worn with a silk blouse, co-ordinated with a straight skirt. The skirt is wool with patch pockets trimmed with fringing and worn with a wide leather belt. A large knitted stole and knitted hat complete the outfit.

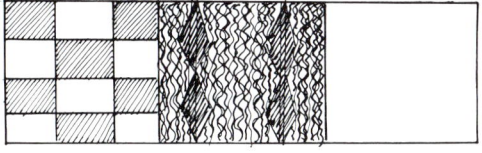

A summer top and skirt in striped cotton lawn. The top is cut very full with a large frill at the neckline and three-quarter length sleeves gathered at the hem. The skirt is full and gathered at the waistband, with a large frill on the hem.

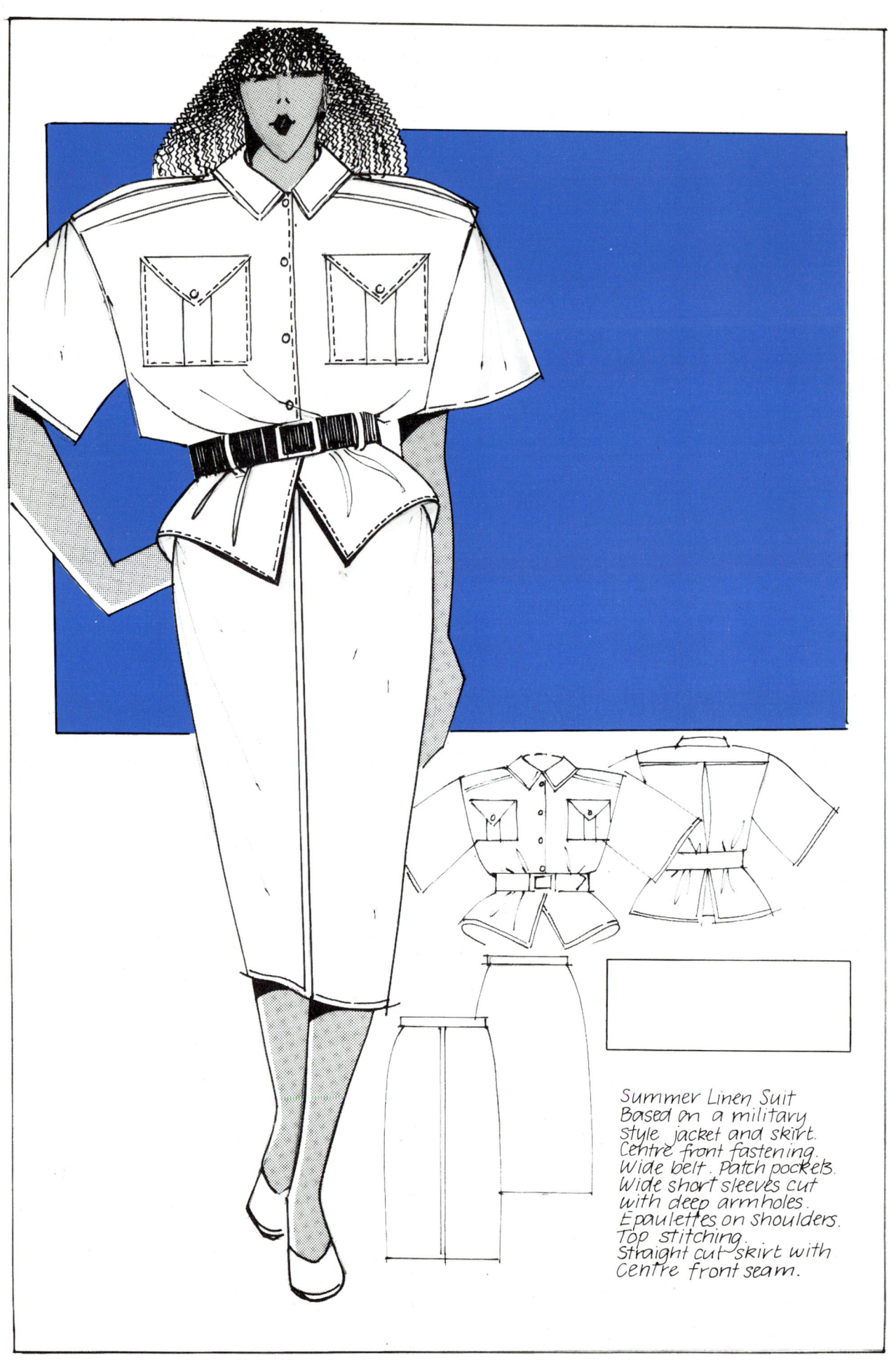

Summer Linen Suit
Based on a military style jacket and skirt. Centre front fastening. Wide belt. Patch pockets. Wide short sleeves cut with deep armholes. Epaulettes on shoulders. Top stitching. Straight cut skirt with centre front seam.

A 1984 summer fashion with a military influence. The drawing was produced with two black fibre tipped pens of different thicknesses, combined with a cool grey magic marker pen for tone effects. The presentation drawing is stylised to project the fashion image. The analytical sketch notes and fabric have been arranged to balance the composition.

Note how the backgrounds suggested in the illustrations have been incorporated with the fashion sketches to complement the design of the garments. The figures can either be sketched on the same sheet as the background or the background can be drawn separately. If drawn separately, the figures should be cut out, placed on the background and fixed with a good adhesive spray or gum (see page 11).

When the drawing is complete it should be mounted on card. Choose a colour and texture of mounting card that will complement the colour you have used in your drawing. (More detail about mounting work is given on page 31.)

Assignment

Keep any cuttings, photographs or sketches of suitable material which could be adapted for background work.

Practise stylised sketches of trees, clouds, boats or buildings etc. Remember that often only an indication of background is necessary to complement the design.

A combination of different line values produced with three felt tipped pens. The tone was added with a grey magic marker and the stripes with watercolour paint. This is a presentation drawing of the design developed on page 8.

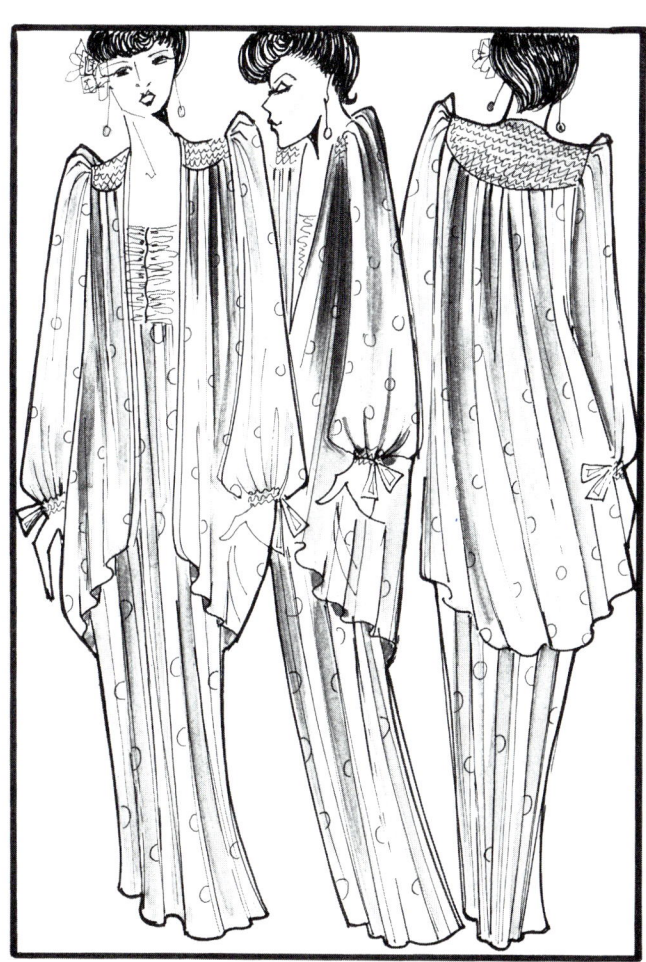

Long dress and coat drawn in Rotring pen and ink with a grey watercolour wash. The darker tones are used to indicate folds and gathers. This is a presentation drawing of the outfit shown in the production drawing on page 23.

Pentel pencil line drawing. The stylised background complements the presentation of the two figures. The accessories help to project the fashion image clearly.

Heads and hairstyles

When drawing figures for presentation sheets it is important that the facial features, make-up and hairstyle of each figure should harmonise with the style of the outfit you have designed and help to promote the desired fashion image.

For sketching heads and hairstyles, it is very important to practise sketching the hair or hat from different angles — back, side and three-quarter views. The hat must be sketched at the correct angle and look as if it really fits the head. Try to make the hairstyle complement the hat. In some instances the hat may completely conceal the hair. The material of the hat should be clearly represented as should any trimmings you choose.

Note the positioning of the features and the guide lines indicating the balance and proportion of the head.

The hats have been constructed round the basic shape of the head and the facial features added to complement the design. When developing your ideas it is not always necessary to sketch facial features in great detail.

Assignment

When possible, practise sketching a selection of hats from a model. Arrange for a friend to model for you or use a millinery block. This will help you considerably when drawing a design from several different angles.

Drawing accessories

As a student, you should practise adding accessories to your fashion design drawings to give the designs a specific fashion image. The shape of a hat, the way in which a necklace is worn or a scarf tied can contribute greatly to the look or mood you are trying to create in your design.

Assignments

1. Make a study of fashion accessories. Note the current trends in shoes, bags, gloves, belts, hats and jewellery. Keep a reference folder of cuttings from newspapers and magazines.
2. Make sketches of a variety of fashion accessories in your sketch book. When drawing shoes sketch the foot shape very lightly in pencil, then draw the shoe round the foot. In some instances it may only be necessary to suggest the style of the shoe in a fashion sketch, indicating the shape with a few simple lines.
3. Make drawings of shoes and boots working from a model. Study pictures of shoes in fashion magazines and look at displays in shop windows for new styles. Try designing some styles of your own.

Mounting and presenting work

It is important when presenting your work for a job or college interview to consider the most effective way of making it easy and enjoyable for the interviewer to look through. Think carefully about which pieces of work you intend to show; your art teacher could probably help you to make the selection. It is a good idea to arrange your work in order, showing the early work first.

Present your design drawings and development sheets in folders which indicate the design brief — fashion theme, season, fabrics etc. Presentation drawings should be mounted. You can mount them in three ways:

Window mounting
Cut the mount out of card with a sharp knife and a steel rule. Fix the drawing at the back of the window mount with adhesive tape.

Flat mounting
Place the drawing on a sheet of card and fix it with an adhesive spray or gum. Make sure before fixing that the drawing is in the correct position. Mark the card with light pencil lines as a guide.

Transparent folders
Place the drawing in a folder, displayed and fixed with gum on a sheet of coloured paper or thin card. Displaying work in this way means that it is protected when handled by examiners or agents. You can display two drawings in one folder as they are double-sided.

It is a good idea to take some free sketches or a sketch book with you to interviews as well as the more finished work. The assessor will be interested to see your methods of working from the first rough sketches to the finished design drawings. If you are applying for a place on a design course it is helpful to take other art work with you: plant and life drawing, paintings, sketches, dressmaking examples and embroidery.

The fashion industry

At several stages during his work on designs for a new collection, the fashion designer will need to consult experts working in other areas of the fashion industry and when the time for marketing new garments arrives the designer or manufacturer needs to use the services of model agencies and retailers to sell his product.

Selecting fabrics

As we saw in the description of the design process (pages 3–5) selecting the fabric is a very important part of a garment's design, which must be carried out at an early stage. A professional designer will make sure he keeps up to date with the new trends in fabrics and to do so he needs to use the advice and expertise of textile manufacturers and consultants.

As a student it is a good idea to make a thorough study of the fabric collections produced by the many textile houses in Britain and abroad. The collections can be viewed in their showrooms or appointments can be made for their representatives to call with samples of a new collection. Many firms specialise in particular fabrics and price ranges, i.e. either in natural fibres — silk, wool, cotton etc. — or in the large range of the man-made fibres.

Designers who work for large manufacturing firms often attend international fashion and textile exhibitions at home and abroad to keep up with the latest trends in fabric design.

Fashion forecast services
There are a number of services a designer can use for advice and information on textiles, colours and the forecast of future fashion trends. In some instances these services are free, others are on subscription. The latter give a more detailed and specialised service in line with your particular requirements, whether they be dresses, coats, children's wear, men's fashions, or sportswear. These services consist of a portfolio which is sent out at regular intervals including information on possible future fashion trends with suggestions of new fashion colours, fabric charts and fashion sketches.

The information is collected and produced by a team of specialists working together, who collate information from all over the world, attending international trade exhibitions and fashion shows. They also visit manufacturers, select fabrics and suggest ways in which colour, pattern and texture can be used.

Fashion shows

Once the designs for a new collection of garments are in production, samples of each design are shown to buyers. Fashion shows are staged and the garments are carefully displayed on rails in the showrooms of wholesale houses and modelled by the house model on request. Sometimes collections are shown to buyers at trade fashion shows in hotels, fashion showrooms, and at exhibitions. The shows are usually organised by model agencies who provide the fashion models.

The fashion buyers from private shops, department stores and chain stores attend the showing of a new collection. Buyers are very familiar with the market for which they are buying. They know which styles, colours and price ranges will sell in particular parts of the country and how to select garments for a variety of markets.

Retail

There is a wide range of retail outlets for clothes ranging from small exclusive shops which buy the more expensive couture clothes, to boutiques, department stores, chain stores and mail order firms which stock lower priced garments. Some manufacturers retail the garments they produce through their own shops; others sell the garments to retailers through wholesale houses. The retailer then sells the clothes in his shops and the designs will be promoted in window displays, advertisements and fashion articles.

Further reading

Costume research

James Snowden: *The Folk Dress of Europe* (Mills & Boon)
M. Tilke: *Costume Patterns and Designs* (Zwemmer)
Angela Bradshaw: *World Costumes* (Black)
Doreen Yarwood: *The Encyclopaedia of World Costume* (Batsford)
Jack Harvey: *Fashion and Clothes* (Macdonald Educational)
Elizabeth Ewing: *Women in Uniform Through the Centuries* (Batsford)
Elizabeth Ewing: *History of Twentieth Century Fashion* (Batsford)
Prudence Glynn with Madeleine Ginsbury: *In Fashion: Dress in the Twentieth Century* (Allen & Unwin)
Julian Robinson: *The Golden Age of Style* (Orbis Publishing)
Pauline Stevenson: *Bridal Fashions* (Ian Allen)
Julian Robinson: *Fashion in the Forties* (Academy Editions)
Jane Dorner: *Fashion in the Twenties and Thirties* (Ian Allen)
Jane Dorner: *Fashion in the Forties and Fifties* (Ian Allen)
John Peacock: *Fashion Sketchbook 1920–1960* (Thames & Hudson)
Designs by 'Erte': Fashion Drawings and Illustrations from 'Harpers Bazaar' (Dover)
Wolfgung Bruhn and Max Tilke: *A Pictorial History of Costume* (Zwemmer)
William Packer: *Fashion Drawing in Vogue* (Thames & Hudson)
Ann Stegemeyer: *Who's Who in Fashion* (Fairchild Publications)
A. Couldridge: *Hatbook* (Batsford)

Fashion drawing

Patrick John Ireland: *Fashion Design Drawing and Presentation* (Batsford)
Patrick John Ireland: *Drawing and Designing Children's and Teenage Fashions* (Batsford)
Patrick John Ireland: *Fashion Design* (Cambridge University Press)

Fashion drawing and anatomy

Joseph Sheppard: *Anatomy* (Pitman)
Don Davy: *Anatomy and Life Drawing* (Blandford Press)
Jack Kramer: *Human Anatomy and Figure Drawing* (Van Nostrand Reinhold)
Joseph Sheppard: *Drawing the Female Figure* (Pitman)
Andrew Ioomis: *Figure Drawing for All Its Worth* (The Viking Portable Library)
Jeno Barcsay: *Anatomy for the Artist* (Octopus)

Magazines

Fashion Forecast (with *Fabric Forecast*)
Fashion Weekly
Harper's and Queen
Harper's Bazaar
Harper's Bazaar Italia
L'Officiel Hommes
L'Officiel Prêt à Porter
Vogue (American)
Vogue (English)
Vogue (French)
Vogue (Italian)
Vogue Bambini